Italian Bakery:

An Italian Bread Cookbook

Lukas Prochazka

Copyright © 2017 Lukas Prochazka
All rights reserved.
ISBN: 154690266X
ISBN-13: 978-1546902669

License Note

No part of this book is permitted to be reproduce in any form or by any means unless a permission is given by its author. All recipes in this book are written only for informative purpose. All readers should be advised to follow the instruction at their own risk.

About the Author

I consider myself to be a very skilled cook and at least good author of many cookbooks, which are now being sold worldwide. I was born in a small town in the north of Czechia. Since very young age I have been drawn to cooking. In 2012 I wrote my first internationally sold cookbook about Czech cuisine. Four years later I republished this book in improved version and since then I have kept on writing new titles. I hope you find my books to be useful and you will get inspiration from these.

For more cookbooks please visit
www.amazon.com/author/prochazkacook

Subscribe on Twitter to stay informed:
www.twitter.com/ProchazkaCook

Contents

About Italian Bread 6

Bossola 8
Ciabatta 9
Ciambella 11
Corenetti 12
Filone 14
Focaccia 16
Focaccia al Pomodoro 18
Friselle 19
Pane alle Olive 20
Pane Casereccio 21
Pane di Genzano 23
Pane Siciliano and Pate Fermentee 24
Pizza Bianca 27
Pumpernickel 28
Rosette 29
Schüttelbrot 31
Taralli 32
Vinschger Paarl 33

Volume Conversion 34
Weights of Common Ingredients 35
Temperature Conversion 36
Length Conversion 37

Italian Bread

What is commonly known as Italian Bread in the World is something like French bread but typically softer. The dough typically contains some olive oil and dairy to soften things up, and instead of steaming the oven to maximize crust you brush the crust with water before placing it in the oven which keeps it softer and chewier. This description fits Focaccia bread, but it is the perfect spongy bread for mopping up pasta sauces, and quite good on its own. But it is just a poor simplification.

Italy is divided into 20 region and every region's bread is quite unique in its own way. Nearer the Alps bread becomes denser and usually consists rye whereas nearer the Sicily bread becomes lighter, softer and oilier.

Rarely is there an Italian meal that does not include bread. Ancient tools and ovens provide proof that man has been making breads for thousands of years. Like many other foods, ancient Romans took the art of bread- making to a higher level. In Latin bread was called "panem", in Italian language it is called "pane".

Italians have high standards for their bread. They are known to allow the yeast to fully rise over the course of several hours, leaving a thin crust. Italians value the size of their loaves of bread because every family member needs to be properly nourished. Italians prefer their bread to have a soft and moist interior, which is ideal for absorbing olive oil, vinegar, tomatoes, and other select toppings. Within the rest of this book you will learn how to make authentic Italian bread.

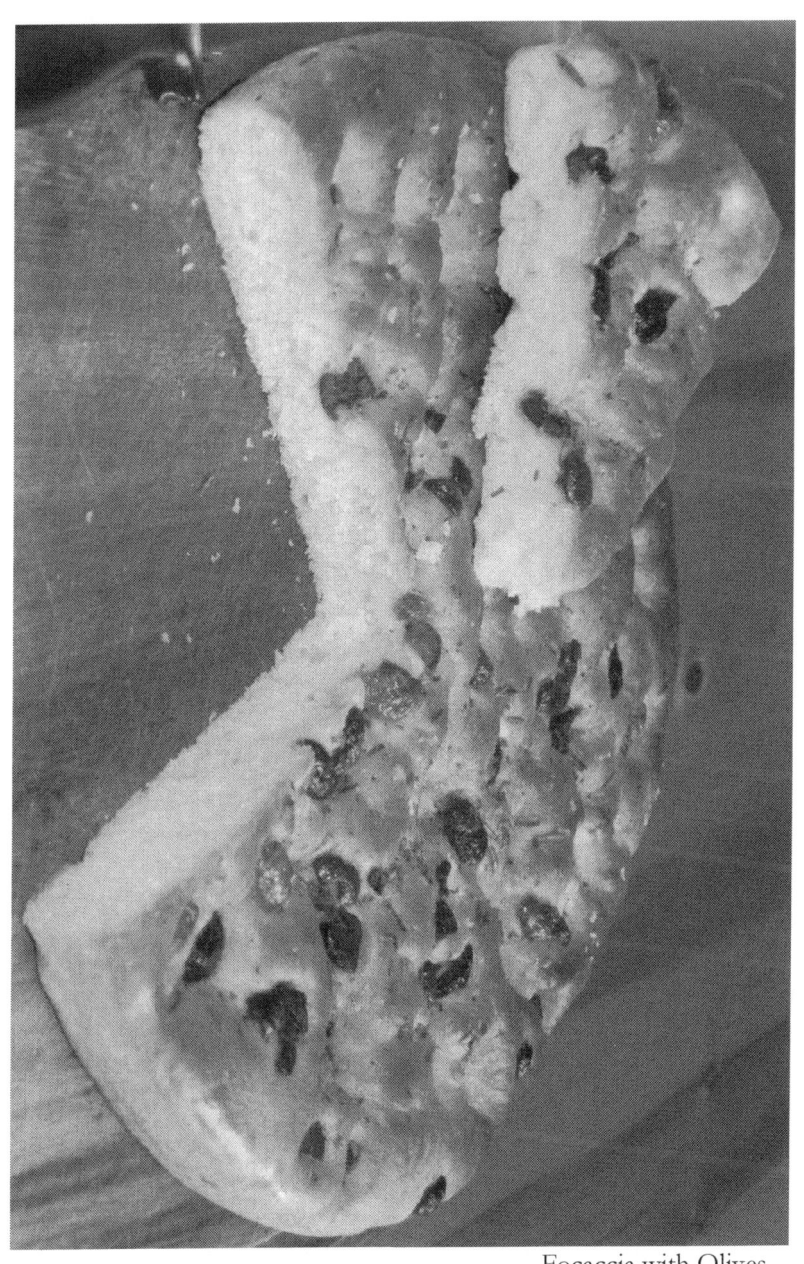

Focaccia with Olives

Bossola

Ingredients:

300g all-purpose flour
100g butter
150g sugar
3 eggs and 1 egg yolk
0.5g vanilla extract
15g baking vanilla
1 pinch of salt
Grains of sugar for garnish

Directions:

1. Preheat oven to 200°C.
2. In a bowl, work the eggs with the flour and salt, add the butter in small pieces, sugar, vanilla and finally the yeast.
3. With the dough so formed a donut worked very well in it and put in a baking pan and sprinkle with flour.
4. Finally surface a beaten egg and sprinkle with sugar grains.
5. Place in preheated oven and bake for about 30 minutes.

Ciabatta

Ciabatte are a flat bread, a bit like pizza Bianca, though harder and made with less oil, good for sandwiches.

Ingredients:

Biga:
1/2 teaspoon active dry yeast
1/4 cup warm water
1 and 1/2 cups water, at room temperature
3 and 3/4 cups unbleached flour
Dough:
1 teaspoon active dry yeast
5 tablespoons warm milk
1 cup water
1 tablespoon olive oil
2 cups biga, rested for 12 hours
3 3/4 cups all-purpose flour
1 tablespoon salt
Cornmeal

Directions:

1. **Biga:** Mix all ingredients and let rest for a day in oiled bowl.
2. **Ciabatta:** Stir the yeast into the milk in a mixer bowl, let stand until creamy, about 10 minutes. Add the water, oil, and biga, mix it well.
3. Mix the flour and salt, add to the bowl, and mix for 2 to 3 minutes. Knead for 5 minutes. The dough will be very sticky.
4. Place the ciabatta dough in an oiled bowl, cover with plastic wrap, and let rise at room temperature until doubled, about 1 and 1/4 hours. The dough should be full of air bubbles, supple, elastic, and sticky.
5. Turn the ciabatta dough onto a generously floured surface and cut it into 4 equal portions. Roll each portion into a cylinder, then stretch each cylinder into a rectangle.

6. Generously flour 4 pieces of parchment paper placed on peels or upside-down baking sheets. Place each loaf, seam side up, on a piece of parchment. Dimple the loaves vigorously with your fingertips or knuckles so that they won't rise too much. The dough will look heavily pockmarked, but it is very resilient, so don't be concerned. Cover the loaves loosely with damp towels and let rise until puffy but not doubled in size, 1 and 1/2 to 2 hours.
7. Preheat oven to 220°C.
8. Just before baking the bread, sprinkle the stones with cornmeal.
9. Bake for a total of 20 to 25 minutes, spraying the oven three times with water in the first 10 minutes.

Ciambella

Ingredients:

400g all-purpose flour
150g margarine
180g sugar
100ml milk
1 pinch salt
4 eggs
1 teaspoon baking powder
1 teaspoon vanilla
2 tablespoons liqueur
1 lemon zest
1-2 tablespoon sugar

Directions:

1. Preheat oven to 220°C.
2. Grease your ring-shaped mold and dust with four.
3. Work all the ingredients. Mix them well.
4. Spread the batter in the mold.
5. Top with sugar.
6. Bake for 30 minutes.

Cornetti

These are similar to French croissants, but sweeter and often filled with a sweet cream or jam, they are a typical Italian breakfast.

Ingredients:

125g bread flour
125g all-purpose flour
4g salt
12g dry yeast
50g whole milk
40ml water
1 egg, lightly beaten
1 vanilla bean
50g caster sugar
30g butter + 125g butter
70g apricot jelly
Zest of one organic orange

Directions:

1. Add the bread flour, the all-purpose flour and salt in the bowl of a stand mixer. Dissolve the yeast in warm milk and add it into the flour, then add the water and the lightly beaten egg. Knead at medium speed for about ten minutes with the hook attachment.
2. Add the 30g butter at room temperature and the sugar mixed with the seeds of the vanilla bean and the grated zest of an orange. Knead for ten minutes with the hook attachment.
3. Remove the dough from the bowl and put it in a plastic bag that has enough space to let it rise and store in the refrigerator for 24 hours.
4. Use the butter at room temperature and with the help of a rolling pin spread it between two sheets of baking paper in a square sheet, as regular as possible. Store in the fridge.
5. The next day, remove the dough from the fridge and turn it on a well-floured work surface. Roll it with a rolling pin on a

disk slightly larger than the butter sheet. Place the butter in the centre of the dough and gently pull the four sides of the dough over the butter, to close it inside as in an envelope.
6. With the help of the rolling pin and other flour stretch the dough so that it could triple its length but maintain the same width.
7. Make a three-fold: divide up the dough into three equal parts and fold on the middle part the right side, then the left one.
8. Seal all the edges by pinching the dough together. Rotate the dough 90 degrees and roll out again in a rectangle sheet so that it quadruples its length
9. Now is the time to give a four-fold: divide up the dough into four equal parts and fold the two outer parts on the two inside. Fold again to close as a book.
10. Wrap the dough in plastic wrap and let it rest in the fridge for an hour.
11. After this time, remove the dough from the refrigerator and roll it into a sheet of 5 mm thickness.
12. With a sharp knife or a pizza wheel cut out strips, then long and narrow triangles. Each triangle should weigh about 50 g.
13. Make a small incision of 1 cm on the short side of the triangle and wrap the triangles on themselves from the short side. Fold the sides of the croissant just formed toward the center, to give a crescent shape, and put the tip of the triangle under the croissant so that it won't open while rising.
14. Arrange the croissants in a tray lined with baking paper and let them rise in a warm place for 2 hours or until they have doubled their volume.
15. Heat oven to 200°C.
16. Bake the croissants for about 15 minutes, until golden brown. In the meantime heat the apricot jelly in the microwave or in a bain-marie with a tablespoon of water. As soon as the croissants are out of the oven brush them with the apricot jelly.

Filone

Ingredients:

Filone:
3 and 3/4 cups all-purpose flour
1 and 1/2 cup of Biga
1 and 1/4 cup water
1 package of active dry yeast
1 tablespoon sugar
2 teaspoons salt

Biga:
1/2 teaspoon active dry yeast
1/4 cup warm water
1 and 1/2 cups water, at room temperature
3 and 3/4 cups unbleached flour

Directions:

1. **Biga:** Mix all ingredients in a bowl.
2. Let the mixture sit in oiled bowl for a day.
3. **Filone:** Mix water and sugar in a large bowl. Add yeast. Allow the mixture to sit for 10 minutes.
4. In a new bowl mix biga and yeast mixture.
5. Next, add the salt and flour and stir well. Knead until the dough is firm doesn't stick.
6. Move the dough to a large, oiled, bowl and cover with both plastic wrap and a large towel. The mixture should be refrigerated for 24 hours.
7. Remove the dough and cut into 3-4 pieces.
8. Roll and flatten the dough on a floured surface, essentially rolling the dough into a log. Place on a covered towel and allow to rise.
9. Preheat oven to 250°C.

10. Make a long incision in the dough and create some moisture in the oven by spraying the oven cavity with water, as well as the shaped dough.
11. Bake for 30 minutes.

Focaccia

The focaccia in Liguria is the Northern brother of the pizza Bianca, a softer crust and a sweeter flavor than Roman pizza Bianca, it resembles bread more than it does pizza.

Ingredients:

1 and 3/4 cups warm water
1 package active dry yeast
1 tablespoon sugar
5 cups all-purpose flour
1 cup extra-virgin olive oil
1 tablespoon kosher salt, plus for sprinkling
Rosemary to garnish

Directions:

1. Combine the warm water, yeast and sugar in a small bowl. Put the bowl in a warm, not hot or cool, place until the yeast is bubbling and aromatic, at least 15 minutes.
2. In the bowl of a mixer fitted with a dough hook, combine the flour, 1 tablespoon of kosher salt, 1/2 cup olive oil and the yeast mixture on low speed. Once the dough has come together, continue to knead for 5 to 6 minutes on a medium speed until it becomes smooth and soft. Give it a sprinkle of flour if the dough is really sticky and tacky.
3. Transfer the dough to a clean, lightly floured surface, then knead it by hand 1 or 2 times.
4. Coat the inside of the mixer bowl lightly with olive oil and return the dough to the bowl. Cover it with plastic wrap and put it in a warm place until the dough has doubled in size, at least 1 hour.
5. Coat a baking pan with the remaining 1/2 cup olive oil.
6. Put the dough onto the baking pan and begin pressing it out to fit the size of the pan. Turn the dough over to coat the other side with the olive oil. Continue to stretch the dough

to fit the pan. As you are doing so, spread your fingers out and make finger holes all the way through the dough.
7. Put the dough in the warm place until it has doubled in size, about 1 hour.
8. Preheat oven to 220°C.
9. Liberally sprinkle the top of the focaccia with some coarse sea salt and lightly drizzle a little oil on top. Bake the dough until the top of the loaf is golden brown, about 25 to 30 minutes.

Focaccia al Pomodoro

Focaccia al Pomodoro can be found in Puglia and in Basilicata, thick crusted dough with fresh tomato sauce baked on top with thyme.

Ingredients:

500g all-purpose flour
225ml water
200g tomato passata
150g mozzarella
70g green olives
70g black olives
1 pack of dried yeast
2 teaspoons sugar
1 teaspoon salt
2 teaspoons olive oil
Salt

Directions:

1. Preheat oven to 200°C.
2. Put the flour in a big bowl and mix it with the yeast. Make a little hole in the middle of the flour and put the sugar, salt and olio in it. Mix it all with the help of a fork, adding the water bits by bits at a time.
3. Work the dough on a slightly floured work basis for at least 10 minutes with your fists.
4. Once you are done, put the dough in a floured container, and cover it with a humid kitchen towel, on a cool and humid place for the dough to rise twice its size.
5. Take the dough out and separate it in two equal pieces and start making two pizza shapes.
6. Spread the passata on top of the dough, then put on equally the mozzarella, olives and salt. You can also add some herbs if you like.
7. Put the focaccia in the middle of the oven for circa 15-20 minutes.

Friselle

Friselle are a dried bread, which vary in thickness and size, depending on what region you are in. Generally eaten with fresh tomatoes, extra virgin olive oil and thyme.

Ingredients:

3 and 1/2 cups all-purpose flour
2 teaspoons baking powder
1 cup olive oil
1 cup cold water
1 teaspoon salt
1 teaspoon ground black pepper

Directions:

1. Preheat oven to 200°C.
2. Whisk flour, baking powder, salt, and black pepper together in a bowl. Stir olive oil and cold water into dry ingredients, mixing to make a soft dough.
3. Pinch off a handful of dough, roll into a thick log between your hands, and use a scissors to cut into pieces about 5cm long.
4. Bake in the preheated oven on middle rack for 15 minutes.
5. Flip biscuits and bake until golden brown on both sides, about 15 minutes more

Pane alle Olive

Ingredients:

500g all-purpose flour
250ml lukewarm water
23g yeast
1 tablespoon olive oil
A pinch of salt
A handful of whole olives, deseeded

Directions:

1. Mix the yeast with a little bit of the flour and some of the water to activate the yeast.
2. When you see bubbles appear in the mixture, add the yeast to the rest of the flour and water a little bit at a time until it comes into a dough. Add the salt and olive oil.
3. Knead for about ten minutes then set the dough in a large bowl.
4. Cover it with plastic wrap and let it rise in a warm place away from draughts for at least one hour.
5. Add the olives, mix through the dough and form into the desired shape.
6. Bake at 200°C for 20 minutes.

Pane Casereccio

Ingredients:

4 cups bread flour
1/2 teaspoon yeast
2 teaspoons salt
2 cups warm water
2 tablespoons extra virgin olive oil
Cornmeal

Directions:

1. Combine the flour, yeast, and salt in a large bowl. Add the water and stir until blended, you'll have a shaggy, sticky dough.
2. Cover the bowl with plastic wrap or put the olive oil in a second large bowl, transfer the dough to that, turn to coat with oil, and cover with plastic wrap. Let the dough rest for about 12-18 hours.
3. Lightly flour a work surface, remove the dough, and fold once or twice; it will be soft but, once sprinkled with flour, not terribly sticky. Cover loosely with plastic wrap and let rest for about 15 minutes.
4. Using just enough flour to keep the dough from sticking, gently and quickly shape the dough into a ball.
5. Generously coat a silicon baking mat or cotton towel with cornmeal; put the dough seam side down on the towel and dust with more flour or cornmeal. Cover with another cotton towel and let rise for about 2 hours. When it's ready, the dough will be more than doubled in size and won't spring back readily when poked with your finger.
6. Preheat oven to 250°C.
7. Put a casserole in the oven.
8. When the dough is ready, carefully remove the pot from the oven and turn the dough over into the pot, seam side up.

9. Cover with the lid and bake for 30 minutes, then remove the lid and bake for another 20 to 30 minutes, until the loaf is beautifully browned.
10. Remove the bread with a spatula or tongs and cool on a rack for at least 30 minutes before slicing.

Pane di Genzano

Ingredients:

1 teaspoon instant yeast
1 and 2/3 cups water
400 grams all-purpose flour
100 grams whole wheat pastry flour
2 teaspoon salt
1/2 cup wheat bran

Directions:

1. Add all of the ingredients except the bran to the bowl of a stand mixer, and mix with the paddle for about two minutes.
2. Switch to the dough hook, and knead for three minutes at low speed, and three minutes and medium speed, or knead by hand.
3. Pour the dough into an oiled bowl, cover with plastic wrap, and place it in a cool place to rise until tripled, about 3 to 5 hours.
4. Lightly oil the bottom of a pie pan and sprinkle the bottom with some of the bran.
5. Shape the dough into a round. Place the round, seam side down, into the pie pan. Sprinkle the top of the dough with the rest of the bran and gently pat it to make sure it sticks.
6. Cover the loaf with oiled plastic wrap or a towel and let rise until doubled, about 2 hours.
7. Preheat oven to 220°C.
8. Place the mold upside down on a baking sheet. Bake for 30 minutes. Remove the mold and bake for additional 15 minutes.

Pane Siciliano and Pate Fermentee

Ingredients:

Pate Fermentee:
1 and 1/8 cups all-purpose flour
1 and 1/8 cups bread flour
3/4 teaspoon salt
1/2 teaspoon instant yeast
3/4 cup water

Pane Siciliano:
1 and 3/4 cups bread flour
1 and 3/4 cups semolina flour
1 and 1/4 teaspoon salt
1 and 1/4 teaspoon instant yeast
2 tablespoons olive oil
1 tablespoon honey
Pate Fermentee
1 and 1/4 cups warm water
Toasted sesame seeds

Directions:

1. **Pate Fermentee:** In the bowl of a stand mixer with a paddle attachment, sift both flours, salt and yeast. Add 3/4 cup of water.
2. Mix on low speed until mixture comes together. If too dry, add additional 2 tablespoons of water a little at a time until mixture is sticky and pulling away from sides of bowl. If more water is needed, add one tablespoon at a time.
3. Trade the paddle for a dough hook and mix the dough for four minutes or knead by hand for six minutes on the counter.

4. Transfer the dough to a bowl with a little bit of olive oil, turning dough so it is covered on all sides.
5. Cover the bowl with plastic wrap and a dish towel and place in a warm location for about 90 minutes.
6. Lightly punch the dough down and then cover. Place in the refrigerator overnight.
7. **Pane Siciliano:** Take Pate Fermentee out of the refrigerator and cut into 10 individuals pieces. Cover with plastic and a towel and let the dough warm up for one hour.
8. In the bowl of a stand mixer with a paddle attachment, sift together both flours, salt and yeast. Add in olive oil, honey, Pate Fermentee pieces and 1 and 1/4 cups of water. Mix it well. Add remaining 1/4 cup of water a teaspoon at a time if needed and only if needed. Dough should be sticky not dry.
9. Knead the dough for 10 minutes.
10. Transfer the dough to a bowl with a little bit of olive oil turning the dough so it is covered on all sides
11. Cover the bowl with plastic wrap and a dish towel and place in a warm place for about two hours or until the dough doubles from its original size.
12. Gently divide the dough into three equal pieces and roll out into three two foot long rolls trying not to degas the dough too much. Press a crease down the center of each roll and fold over and seal as if you were sealing and envelope ending with seam side down. If dough is not pliable enough, let rest for five minutes then continue. You want the dough to stretch and stay stretched and not bounce back or pull back.
13. Roll each end around pinwheel style towards the center. Each end should roll in the opposite direction of the other end so it forms the letter S.
14. Sprinkle two sheet pans with a little semolina flour and place two loaves of dough on one pan and the third in the center of the other pan. Leave enough room for the bread to double in size.
15. Mist the top of each dough with water and sprinkle sesame seeds over.
16. Preheat oven to 250°C.
17. Working quickly, place the bread dough onto the middle rack and pour a cup of hot water into the pan at the bottom of the oven and close the door. After 30 seconds, spray the

oven walls with the mister and close the door. Repeat twice more at 30 second intervals.
18. After the final spray, lower the oven temperature to 220°C and bake for 15 minutes. Rotate the pan 180 degrees. At this point, if the loaves are touching, separate them slightly.
19. Bake for another 10-15 minutes more until the loaves are rich and golden brown all over. If there are still white parts, extend the baking time a few extra minutes.
20. Remove the pans and transfer the bread to a cooling rack and cool for 45 minutes.

Pizza Bianca

This type of bread is typical all over Italy, it is only called pizza Bianca in Rome and of course the way that it is made and the way that it tastes is different in every region. Bakers will often offer small pieces to children while their parents are buying bread. It is wonderful on its own and can also be filled or farcita and made into a sandwich.

Ingredients:

3 cups all-purpose flour
1 teaspoon salt
3/4 teaspoon sugar
1 teaspoon instant dry yeast
3 tablespoons extra-virgin olive oil
1 sprig fresh rosemary

Directions:

1. Combine flour, 1/2 teaspoon salt, sugar, and yeast in the bowl of an electric mixer, and slowly add 1 cup cold water.
2. Mix for about 10 minutes until the dough is smooth, elastic, and cleanly pulls away from the sides of the mixing bowl.
3. Place dough in an oiled bowl, and allow to rest for 2 to 4 hours until it has doubled in size.
4. Split the dough into halves, and form each into a log. Place each log on a generously floured surface, and allow it to rest until the formed dough doubles in size again, at least 1 hour.
5. Shape each log to be 1 cm thick rectangle.
6. Preheat oven to 250°C and let the dough rest again. Drizzle with remaining olive oil, rosemary and sprinkle with remaining salt.
7. When oven reaches desired temperature bake for 12 minutes.

Pumpernickel

Ingredients:

3 and 1/4 cups bread flour
1 and 1/3 cups rye flour
2 cups warm milk
2 tablespoons vegetable oil
4 tablespoons molasses
1/2 cup cornmeal
1 and 1/3 teaspoons salt
2 and 2/3 teaspoons active dry yeast
4 tablespoons cocoa powder
2 and 2/3 tablespoons brown sugar

Directions:

1. Mix well bread flour, rye flour, cornmeal, salt, yeast, cocoa, and brown sugar. Add milk, oil, and molasses.
2. Mix thoroughly. When mixed well enough that the dough holds together, knead by hand 15-20 minutes.
3. Cover, let rise in bowl 30 minutes. Punch down, form, and place into a pan. Cover with damp cloth and let rise about 1 hour.
4. Preheat oven to 180°C.
5. Bake for 30 minutes.

Rosette

Ingredients:

Biga:
400g all-purpose flour
175 g water
4g fresh yeast
Dough:
Biga
40g all-purpose flour
55g water
4g sugar
8g salt

Directions:

1. **Biga:** Mix roughly.
2. Cover and leave for 16 – 20 hours.
3. **Dough:** Dissolve sugar in water and mix into the biga, then add the flour and mix for 6 minutes.
4. Flatten out and shape into a bowl, cover and leave for 10 – 15 minutes.
5. Roll out on a floured board.
6. Fold the dough 2 times.
7. Cover and leave for 15 minutes.
8. Roll out and fold again.
9. Cover and leave for 15 minutes
10. Cover with a little oil.
11. Leave for 30 minutes
12. Divide into quarters and then into eighths.
13. Roll into balls on floured board and then flatten.
14. Then do special fold four corners, like gathering a napkin, trying to keep air in the centre of the ball, pinch together and then turn over, and gently shape into balls with a cupped hand, rotating on a clean worktop.
15. Leave balls for 30 minutes.

16. Dust the tops with flour
17. Then cut them with the Rosette press, or like Vittorio, use an apple cutter, almost all the way through. Pick up ball of dough, turn over and tuck the corners into ball shape
18. Place cut side down on a floured tray.
19. Cover and leave for 45 – 60 minutes
20. Preheat oven to 250°C.
21. Add baking pan of water on the bottom of oven.
22. Open for 5 seconds when the oven heats up.
23. Bake for 20 – 25 minutes.

Schüttelbrot

The bread in Alto-Adige is a lot like the bread that you can find in Germany and Austria, culturally Alto-Adige is Austrian since it only became a part of Italy after the First World War. This is a hard and crispy rye bread.

Ingredients:

100g wholemeal flour
250g rye flour
350g wheat flour
250ml water
250ml milk
3 teaspoon caraway seeds
30g yeast
1 pinch salt
1 teaspoon sugar
4 teaspoon oil
1 egg

Directions:

1. Mix different flour types together in a bowl and make a small dent in the middle.
2. Pour water into another bowl, add sugar and stir.
3. Pour this mixture into the hollow in the flour, sprinkle salt around the hollow, add milk and other ingredients and mix everything together.
4. Allow to rise for around 25 minutes.
5. Form small balls from dough and roll out into rounds of about 5 mm thickness with a rolling pin.
6. Place on baking tray, beat egg and brush onto dough. Allow to rise for another 15 minutes.
7. Bake for 5 to 10 minutes.

Taralli

Ingredients:

700g all-purpose flour
250ml extra-virgin olive oil
250ml lukewarm water
Splash red wine

Directions:

1. Preheat oven to 200°C.
2. Place the flour on a worktable. Make a well in the center of the flour and add the olive oil, wine and water. Combine the ingredients and knead until the mixture becomes an even dough.
3. Cut off a small amount of dough and roll into a 1cm thick log. Cut the log into 12cm long pieces.
4. Then form a doughnut-like shape by pinching the opposite ends together. Repeat the above process with the remaining dough.
5. Place the taralli in a pot of boiling water for about 1 minute or until they float to the surface. Stir to prevent them from sticking together.
6. Remove the taralli from the water with a slotted spoon and dry off any excess water with a dishcloth.
7. Line a baking tray with parchment paper and bake for approximately 10 minutes or until golden brown on one side.

Vinschger Paarl

This bread originates in northern Italy. As focaccia vinschger is a flat bread.

Ingredients:

220g rye flour
200ml lukewarm water
5g fresh yeast
500g rye flour
280g wheat flour
20g fresh yeast dissolved in 700 ml lukewarm water
20g salt
10g fennel
5g cumin seeds

Directions:

1. Dissolve the yeast in warm water, mix well with the flour, and keep stirring for 5 min.
2. Cover with cheesecloth and leave in a warm place for 1 hour.
3. Mix the sourdough with the other ingredients to form a soft dough.
4. Dust with rye flour and leave for 10-15 min.
5. Divide into 10 pieces of similar size and form small rolls.
6. Allow to swell for 30-45 min.
7. Bake for 45 minutes.

Volume Conversion

Customary Quantity	Metric Equivalent
1 teaspoon	5 ml
1 tablespoon	15ml
1/8 cup	30 ml
1/4 cup	60 ml
1/3 cup	80 ml
1/2 cup	120 ml
2/3 cup	160 ml
3/4 cup	180 ml
1 cup	240 ml
1 1/2 cups	360 ml
2 cups	480 ml
3 cups	720 ml
4 cups	960 ml

Weights of Common Ingredients

Ingredient	1 cup	1/2 cup	2 Tbs
Flour	120 g	70 g	15 g
Sugar	200 g	100 g	25 g
Rice	190 g	100 g	24 g
Macaroni	140 g	70 g	17 g
Butter	240 g	120 g	30 g
Chopped Nuts	150 g	75 g	20 g
Bread Crumbs	150 g	75 g	20 g
Grated Cheese	90 g	45 g	11 g

Temperature Conversion

Fahrenheit	Celsius
250	120
275	140
300	150
325	160
c350	180
375	190
400	200
425	220
450	203

Length Conversion

Inch	cm
0,125	0,32
0,25	0,63
0,5	1,27
1	2,54
2	5,08
5	12,7

Thank you, my dearest reader, for investing time and money to read this book!

The stores all full of many books dedicated to cooking either collecting and sharing recipes or presenting new ones. I sincerely thank you for choosing this very book and reading it to its very end.

I hope you have enjoyed this book as much as possible and that you have learnt something new and interesting. If you have enjoyed this book, please take a few minutes to write a review summarizing your thoughts and opinion on this book.

If you are interested in other paperback books of mine check out my official amazon author's profile:

www.amazon.com/author/prochazkacook

Besides printed book Amazon offers eBook as well, but if you do not enjoy Amazon's Kindle, my books can be found in other stores such as Kobo.com, Lulu.com, or even iBook for Apple devices.

Thanks for buying this books and have best of luck.

Sincerely,

Lukas Prochazka

Learn more about European cuisines

If you are interested in other European cuisines you should consider checking out the other ethnical cookbooks.

Every ethnical cookbook is followed by a small brochure focused on an aspect typical for the cuisine of the country.

Czech cuisine is regarded as one of the best cuisine by the experts yet it gets little attention. Learn how to make genuine Czech meal.

If you want to learn more about Czech pubs and the meal served in those, check out the Czech Pub Food cookbook.

German, an unrepeatable neighbour of Czechia, is a country with the huge national heritage including the cuisine. German cuisine greatly influenced the cuisine of the United States, especially the most popular food, hamburger.

German Eintopf is most of times regarded as a cooking joke, but it can be tasty. Learn more about this iconic German meal.

Made in United States
Orlando, FL
14 June 2025